CATASTROPHE!

AIR
DISASTERS

John Hawkins

Published in 2012 by The Rosen Publishing Group, Inc.
29 East 21st Street, New York, NY 10010

Author: John Hawkins
Editors: Joe Harris and Penny Worms
Design: Graham Rich
Cover design: Graham Rich

Picture credits:
Corbis: cover, 1, 4, 5, 6b, 7, 8, 9, 16, 19, 20, 24b, 27, 28b, 31, 34, 42, 45t, 45bc. Getty: 10b, 11, 12, 13, 14b, 23, 33, 37, 38, 39, 41, 44 (all), 45tc. Shutterstock: 6t, 10t, 14t, 18t, 22t, 24t, 26, 28t, 30t, 32t, 36t, 40.

Cover image: Naha Airport, Okinawa, Japan. Inspectors look at the remains of the left wing engine of a China Airlines Boeing 737 on August 20, 2007. Fire broke out after the plane landed, but all 157 passengers and eight crew members evacuated safely.

Library of Congress Cataloging-in-Publication Data

Hawkins, John.
  Air disasters / John Hawkins. — 1st ed.
      p. cm. — (Catastrophe!)
  Includes bibliographical references and index.
  ISBN 978-1-4488-6006-7 (library binding)
1. Aircraft accidents—Juvenile literature. 2. Disasters—Juvenile literature. I. Title.
  TL553.5.H41 2012
  363.12′4--dc23
                                              2011015169
Printed in China
SL001925US

CPSIA Compliance Information: Batch #W12YA. For further information, contact Rosen Publishing, New York, New York, at 1-800-237-9932.

Contents

What Happens in an Air Crash?

When a plane crashes, it's vital that help is at hand quickly. Fire can spread quickly through a plane. However, if firefighters can control the fire, the passengers inside have a better chance of escaping.

DANGER ZONE

The majority of aircraft accidents happen during takeoff or landing. For this reason airports around the world have their own fire services, ready to deal with any emergency.

DRILLS

Airport fire crews know that they must be ready at any time of day or night if a plane has a problem. This is why they constantly practice their drills.

Opposite: Airport firefighters at Narita International Airport in Chiba, Japan, put out a fire on a cargo plane.

RAPID RESPONSE

Airport trucks can be at the site of a crash, pumping foam into a fire within two minutes of an emergency call. However, the farther away the crash is, the slower the response.

CRASH INVESTIGATORS

After a crash, it is essential to find out why the accident happened, so that airports, aircraft designers, and governments can make plans to ensure that similar accidents do not happen in future. After a plane crash, the wreckage is left in place for accident investigators to examine and photograph. It is their job to work out what went wrong.

After a collision between a small private aircraft and an airliner in California, accident investigators examine the remains of a plane.

The 9/11 Hijacking, 2001

September 11, 2001 was a turning point in recent history. It was the date of the most infamous plane crashes in history. These crashes were not accidents, but deliberate acts of terrorism. Hijackers used planes as missiles, flying them into buildings. Thousands of people lost their lives on that day.

AN ORDINARY DAY

September 11, 2001 began as a beautiful sunny morning. New York commuters were making their way to work. About 50,000 people entered the Twin Towers of the World Trade Center. American Airlines Flights 11 and 175 took off from Boston, Flight 77 from Washington, and Flight 93 left Newark.

As the North Tower was burning, a second plane crashed into the South Tower of the World Trade Center.

SHOCK ATTACK

Just before 8:46 AM a Boeing 767 (Flight 11) appeared low in the sky above Manhattan, flying at 466 mph (750 kph). New Yorkers watched in horror as it smashed into the North Tower of the World Trade Center, between the 93rd and 99th floors. A huge explosion erupted.

FIRST IMPACT

All the passengers, including the hijackers, died instantly. Hundreds of people working in the tower were killed by the impact. The force of the blast made the tower rock from side to side. People inside heard loud grinding noises as the walls of the tower were put under enormous stress.

Rescue workers walk through the rubble of the Twin Towers.

EYEWITNESS

Fire chief Peter Hayward was involved with planning the response to the fires on the North Tower. "We had a large volume of fire on the upper floors. Each floor was approximately an acre in size. Several floors of fire would have been beyond the fire-extinguishing capability of the forces we had on hand. So we determined, very early on, that this was going to be strictly a rescue mission."

USA, 2001

THE SOUTH TOWER IS HIT

Seventeen minutes after the first collision, while New Yorkers were still trying to understand what had just happened, Flight 175 hit the South Tower. The impact destroyed four floors. The intense fires burning in the towers weakened the steel framework of the building.

COLLAPSE

The fires caused the floors to sag, pulling the outer columns inward. The columns could no longer support the buildings. The South Tower collapsed at 9:59 AM and the North Tower collapsed at 10:28 AM. About 2,750 people were killed in the attack on the Twin Towers, including 345 firefighters and 60 police officers.

A helicopter hovers over the Pentagon, inspecting the damage caused by the third hijacked plane.

A "tribute in lights" shines into the New York sky on the eighth anniversary of the attacks.

WHY DID IT HAPPEN?

The planes had been hijacked by terrorists. The terrorists took over the controls and deliberately flew the planes into buildings full of people. They were linked to Al-Qaeda, a terrorist group based in Afghanistan. Members of Al-Qaeda believe that Muslims are engaged in a holy war against Western countries such as the United States. As a result of the 9/11 terrorist attacks in 2001, the United States, together with a coalition of other countries, launched an invasion of Afghanistan in October 2001.

FLIGHT 77

At 9:40 AM Flight 77 crashed into the Pentagon. The 64 people on board all died, as did 125 people in the building.

HEROES

The fourth plane never reached its target, which was probably the White House. Instead, Flight 93 crashed in Pennsylvania. This was a direct result of the heroic efforts of passengers on board, who fought back against the terrorists detaining them.

CANARY ISLANDS

The Tenerife Collision, 1977

The world's worst airplane accident took place on the ground at Rodeos Airport on Tenerife in the Canary Islands on March 27, 1977. Two Boeing 747s collided with each other on the runway.

FOG-BOUND COLLISION

A KLM jet was speeding down the fogbound runway to take off and ran into a Pan Am plane, on charter from Los Angeles, which was taxiing into position. All 248 passengers and crew on board the KLM jumbo were killed instantly, along with 326 people on the Pan Am plane. The death toll eventually climbed to 583 people in all.

Tenerife was the world's worst ever airplane accident.

FAILURE TO COMMUNICATE

It is thought that the accident was caused by a misunderstanding in the use of English. The KLM pilot misunderstood what the air traffic controller had said and thought he had been given clearance to take off.

Only fragments of the planes were recognizable.

LOST IN TRANSLATION

A similar misunderstanding caused a crash in New York in January 1990. An Avianca Boeing 707 was *en route* from Medellín in Colombia to New York's JFK Airport. The 707 was circling in mid-air (in a holding pattern) while waiting to be given permission to land. The plane was low on fuel. However, the crew was unable to explain the urgent fuel problem to air traffic control. Due to bad weather the crew had to abandon an attempted landing. Soon afterward the fuel ran out completely, and the plane crashed into woods. In all, 73 out of the 158 passengers and crew were killed by the crash.

MOUNTAIN CRASH

The Tenerife crash is not the only misunderstanding to end in catastrophe. In December 1995, an American Airlines plane, traveling from Miami, crashed into a mountain in Cali, Colombia, while descending. In all, 163 passengers and crew members were killed in the collision. The air traffic controller knew that the information he had been given by the flight crew did not match his instructions. However, the controller and crew did not have a common language. He could not ask the pilot to explain.

Amazingly, 70 people survived the initial Tenerife crash.

Tenerife, 1977: one jet engine sits almost undamaged in the wreckage.

ECHOES OF TENERIFE

On October 8, 2001, a crash in Milan claimed more than 110 lives. The accident bears a chilling resemblance to the 1977 disaster in Tenerife. An SAS jet took off while a German Cessna was taxiing on the runway in thick fog. Milan Airport's ground radar system was out of action. The SAS pilot was accelerating toward takeoff when the Cessna suddenly loomed out of the fog.
He appears to have swerved at the last minute, but by then a collision was unavoidable. Both planes were wrecked and scores of people died.

LEARNING FROM CATASTROPHES

The International Civil Aviation Organization (ICAO) is a body created by the United Nations to oversee international air travel. It is responsible for setting safety standards. Until December 2008, air traffic controllers did not have to be able to speak good English. However they did have to be able to communicate using the standard ICAO radio codes. The ICAO has now changed its rules about language to protect people from confusion that can lead to disasters. Since December 2008, all air traffic controllers must be skilled at speaking English.

Antarctic Volcano Collision, 1979

At 8:20 AM on November 28, 1979, Flight 901 left Auckland Airport in New Zealand on an eleven-hour sightseeing flight over Antarctica. This was the last journey the 237 passengers and 20 crew would ever take.

A FATAL MISTAKE

Captain Jim Collins and his copilot Greg Cassin had not flown over Antarctica before. However, the DC-10's computerized navigation system was programmed to keep the plane on course. Collins and Cassin did not realize that the longitude and latitude coordinates had been changed. This moved the flight path of the aircraft 30 miles (48 km) to the east.

A DC-10 plane waits on an airport runway.

Ash pours from Mount Erebus.

HIDDEN VOLCANO

Once over Antarctica, Collins flew low to give his passengers a better view. But Flight 901 was not flying above McMurdo Sound, as he thought. It was in fact flying across Lewis Sound towards Mount Erebus, a 12,500 foot (3,810 m) high active volcano. The snow-covered mountain was invisible against the white background of Antarctic ice.

SIX-SECOND WARNING

At 12:49 PM the deck altitude alarm sounded, but there was no time for the pilots to react. Six seconds later Flight 901 hit the side of Mount Erebus and disintegrated. The wreckage left a 2,000-foot (610 m) trail across the lower slopes of Mount Erebus. The fuel tanks exploded. A fireball ripped through the fuselage. All 257 people on board died. The plane was so far off its flight path that it took a rescue party 20 hours to find it.

AFTER THE CRASH

The task of recovering and identifying the bodies of the passengers and crew was difficult because of the numbers involved. More than 60 people worked on the accident site, most in body recovery.

The interior of the DC-10 was spacious by modern standards.

THE VICTIMS

On board the plane had been New Zealanders and foreign nationals. There were 24 Japanese, 22 Americans, six British, two Canadians, one Australian, one Frenchman, and one Swiss. In all, 213 victims were eventually identified, but 44 were mutilated beyond recognition.

MECHANICAL FAULTS?

Early in the investigation into the causes of the disaster, it became clear that there was no mechanical reason for the crash. The flight recorder tapes showed there had been no emergency in the cockpit of the aircraft.

HUMAN ERROR

The inquiry placed the blame on the pilots' inexperience, and the airline systems that allowed the aircraft to be programmed to fly on the path which led directly to Mount Erebus.

REMEMBERING THE DEAD

A wooden cross was erected above Scott Base to commemorate the disaster. In 1986 it was replaced with an aluminum cross after the original one was eroded by ice and snow. The Mount Erebus disaster remains New Zealand's biggest single tragedy, with one more death than in the Napier Earthquake of 1931.

 EYEWITNESS

Inspector Jim Morgan led the team recovering bodies from the wreckage.

"The fact that we all spent about a week camped in polar tents amid the wreckage and dead bodies, maintaining a 24-hour work schedule says it all. We split the men into two shifts (12 hours on and 12 off), and recovered with great effort all the human remains at the site. Many bodies were trapped under tons of fuselage and wings and much physical effort was required to dig them out and extract them."

America's Worst Air Crash, 1979

On May 25, 1979, an American Airlines DC-10 took off from O'Hare International Airport in Chicago. The plane reached a height of 400 feet (122 m) before the thrust of takeoff tore the left-hand engine off the wing.

MEMORIAL DAY WEEKEND

American Airlines Flight 191 was on its way to Los Angeles. Nearly every seat was filled as it was the start of the Memorial Day weekend. On board were 271 people. Soon after 3 PM Central Standard Time, the DC-10 was cleared by O'Hare tower for takeoff.

TAKEOFF

The plane carried a heavy load of jet fuel for its 1,700-mile (2,735 km) flight. It thundered down the runway and lifted off. But the moment it took to the air, the port engine fell from the wing. It fell to the ground, and skidded to the end of the runway.

ENGINE LOSS

With one engine missing, the plane was in desperate trouble and it began to roll sharply to the left. The control tower radioed the captain Walter Lux and asked if he wanted clearance for an emergency landing. There was no response.

PLUMMETING TO THE GROUND

Less than a minute after takeoff, the plane smashed into the ground and caught fire about a half mile (0.8 km) from the end of the runway. All on board were killed, as well as two people on the ground.

This was the scene near O'Hare International Airport after the crash.

Crash investigators inspect the wreckage of Flight 191.

AN INFERNO

The inferno after the crash was so intense that firefighters and rescue personnel could not get near it. The flames and smoke from the wreckage reached twice the height of the plane at its highest.

CRASH INVESTIGATION

Crash investigators from the National Transportation Safety Board pieced together hundreds of pieces of the wreckage.

LOSS OF CONTROL

Experts agreed that it would have been impossible to control the plane once an engine had fallen off, especially during takeoff. No blame was attached to the pilots as there was no possibility they could have recovered the situation.

DESIGN FLAWS

After the crash, all DC-10s were grounded. Inspectors found similar weaknesses in the engine attachments of other planes. These could have had catastrophic results.

LEARNING FROM CATASTROPHES

Crash investigators from the National Transportation Safety Board concluded that factors contributing to the cause of the accident included "the vulnerability of the design of the pylon attach points to maintenance damage; the vulnerability of the design of the leading edge slat system to the damage which produced asymmetry; deficiencies in Federal Aviation Administration surveillance and reporting systems which failed to detect the use of improper maintenance procedures; deficiencies in the practices and communications among operators, the manufacturer, and the FAA... and the intolerance of prescribed operational procedures to this unique emergency."

PARIS

Sucked into the Air, Paris, 1974

On March 3, 1974, 346 people died needlessly when a McDonnell Douglas DC-10 operated by Turkish Airlines crashed into a forest outside Paris. The cargo door had not been properly closed.

A GAPING HOLE

As the plane gained altitude, the cargo door blew off. This caused the cargo compartment to decompress. The floor above the cargo compartment gave way. Six passengers still strapped to their seats were sucked out of the gaping hole to their deaths.

COLLAPSED FLOOR

The remaining passengers had only a few seconds more to live. The collapsed floor had jammed the control lines to the tail. This made it impossible to fly the plane. 72 seconds after the cargo door blew off, the plane crashed, killing everyone on board.

Paris was in shock in the wake of the accident.

WHY DID IT HAPPEN?

It never should have happened. After the accident an inquiry was held. A cargo loader revealed that he had had trouble closing the cargo doors on the DC-10. Little had been done to fix this problem before the Paris crash.

Two years before, the cargo door had blown off an American Airlines DC-10 flying from Detroit to Buffalo. However, Captain Bryce McCormick and First Officer Peter Witney had managed to land the damaged aircraft safely. Nobody was harmed. In fact, on that occasion, the only "casualty" was a corpse in a coffin. The coffin was sucked out of the open door and fell from a great height.

Indian Collision, 1996

At around 6:40 PM on November 13, 1996, the radar blips of two aircraft disappeared from the air traffic controllers' radar screens at New Delhi's Indira Gandhi International Airport. A nightmarish mid-air collision had taken place.

Officials inspect the wreckage of one of the planes after the mid-air collision.

CRASH COURSE

At 6:32 AM, a Saudi 747 with 312 passengers aboard took off from New Delhi's Indira Gandhi International Airport. It was heading for Saudi Arabia. The plane was cleared to climb to 14,000 feet (4,267 m). Meanwhile a Kazakh Ilyushin Il-76 cargo plane with 38 crew was told to descend to 15,000 feet (4,572 m) on its approach to the airport.

GIANT FIREBALLS

In cloudy skies about 60 miles (97 km) to the west of New Delhi, over the village of Charkhi Dadri, the two planes collided. Two giant fireballs turned the sky red.

BLOWN APART

Wreckage, baggage, and body parts were scattered across six miles (9.7 km) of wheat and mustard fields near the village of Charkhi Dadri. The first people to arrive at the scene said the air was filled with the smell of burning flesh.

UNRECOGNIZABLE VICTIMS

One of them, 19-year-old college student Manjit Singh, saw 60 or 70 bodies, but said that only about 15 were identifiable. The faces of the rest were horribly charred. Some 200 bodies were collected from the fields. Nothing remained of the other 150 people on board.

EYEWITNESS

The pilot of a U.S. Air Force transport plane carrying supplies for the American Embassy in New Delhi witnessed the crash from 20,000 feet (6,096 m). "We noticed out of our right-hand (side of the plane) a large cloud lit up with an orange glow, from within the clouds. The glow intensity of the cloud became dimmer and the two fireballs descended and became fireballs on the ground."

BADEN-WÜRTTEMBERG

Lake Constance Collision, 2002

A similar accident occurred over southern Germany on July 2, 2002, when another Russian Tupolev 154 airliner carrying 95 people collided with a Boeing 757 cargo aircraft operated by the courier company DHL and carrying a crew of three.

THE FLIGHTS

The Tupolev was flying from Moscow to Barcelona, while the Boeing was flying from Bergamo in Italy to Brussels. They were under the control of Swiss air traffic control at the time of the accident.

FLAMES FROM THE SKY

The crash happened shortly before midnight at 35,000 feet (10,668 m) above the state of Baden-Württemberg.

Witnesses described seeing two large balls of flames fall from the sky and wreckage from the crash was spread over a 25-mile (40-km) area.

EMERGENCY SERVICES

Police radio reported that bodies were lying everywhere. Police call centers were jammed with calls about the crash. Emergency services from across southern Germany were called in.

Relatives of Russian victims visit the site of the plane crash.

SET ON FIRE

A farm, a school, and several houses near the town of Überlingen on the banks of Lake Constance, close to the Swiss and Austrian borders, were set on fire by the falling debris.

Two bodies were found among the debris on a road in the village of Owingen on the Bodensee, the resort area of Lake Constance. Other bodies fell into the lake itself.

EYEWITNESS

"I saw the planes hit," said one witness. "There was a huge orange fireball. There are bodies on the ground across this massive slaughter field. People are looking on simply shocked. They are searching with spotlights, looking through a field of death. It seems a hopeless task."

KINSHASA

Kinshasa Crash, 1996

At least 250 people were killed when a cargo plane crashed into a crowded street market in Kinshasa, capital of Zaire (now the Democratic Republic of the Congo) on January 8, 1996. The plane burst into flames on impact. Most of the victims were women and children shopping at the market.

Crowds of people shop at a busy street market in Kinshasa.

TRAPPED ON THE GROUND

The Antonov 32 cargo plane simply failed to get airborne. Witnesses said it got only a few feet off the ground before crashing.

CRUSHED BENEATH ITS WHEELS

It continued on the ground straight across the street at the end of the runway into the market. The market was in a shanty town made from wood and corrugated iron. The plane plowed on through the market for about a hundred yards (90 m) before stopping. It left a trail of dead and injured people.

CASUALTIES

A fire crew from the airport rushed to the scene to fight the flames. Between 40 and 60 injured people were treated at the scene, but rescue efforts were hampered by people who descended on the downtown airport in search of their relatives. The four Russian crew members, who survived the crash, were arrested.

 WHY DID IT HAPPEN?

It is thought that the plane had failed to get airborne because it was overloaded. Another overloaded plane had also crashed the previous month. The Lockheed Electra passenger plane was owned by a private Zairean firm. It crashed in Angola, killing 141 people. There were few regulations in Zaire to prevent such disasters occurring. Years of civil war and neglect had left the the road network in Zaire a shambles. For this reason, hundreds of small private airline companies had sprung up. These companies provided a means of travel across the vast African country. However, they were not always safe.

Mid-Atlantic Crash, 1996

A Trans World Airlines jumbo jet bound for Paris crashed into the Atlantic Ocean on July 17, 1996. The plane crashed about a half hour after leaving Kennedy Airport in New York. All 230 people on board flight TWA 800 were killed in the collision.

BALL OF FLAMES

Witnesses described seeing two explosions, and then a bright red fireball falling into the ocean. The plane appeared to break into two pieces before disappearing into the sea.

WAS IT TERRORISM?

At first, federal officials thought the crash had been caused by a bomb, although they found no evidence for this. They also looked into the possibility that the plane had been struck by a missile. This was because an unexplained blip appeared on radar screens just before the crash, and witnesses had seen a streak of light moving toward the plane. But the plane was flying too high to be hit by conventional ground-to-air missiles.

This image shows the partially reassembled wreckage of TWA Flight 800.

WAS IT THE MILITARY?

In September 2000, a new theory was put forward. It was suggested that TWA 800 was downed by electromagnetic pulses from military craft. The plane was flying at a time when military exercises involving submarines and U.S. Navy P-3 fighter planes were taking place. It has been suggested that strong electromagnetic pulses generated by military machinery could have caused a mechnical failure.

WHY DID IT HAPPEN?

National Transportation Safety Board Vice Chairman Robert Francis concluded that "there is no evidence at this point that this is not an accident." The most likely explanation was that a catastrophic mechanical failure had ignited the 250,000 pounds (113 tonnes) of fuel on the plane.

GONESSE

Concorde Disaster, 2000

At 4:42 PM on July 25, 2000, Concorde Flight AF4590 was cleared for takeoff at Charles de Gaulle Airport in Paris. One minute and 13 seconds later, the control tower radioed the crew the alarming message: "You have flames, you have flames behind you." But the crew could do nothing to fight the devastating fire.

ENGINE TROUBLE

The Air France plane had been chartered by a German tour operator to take German tourists to New York to join a cruise ship bound for Ecuador. The pilots had already detected a problem with engine two under the left wing and shut it down. They made a desperate attempt to gain height.

Meanwhile the control tower cleared Concorde to make an emergency landing at nearby Le Bourget Airport.

MID-AIR EXPLOSION

With airspeed warnings and fire alarms sounding in the background, pilot Christian Marty said simply: "Too late... no time."

Concorde crashed minutes after takeoff, flames trailing behind the craft.

CRASHDOWN

Seconds later, the plane hit the ground near the town of Gonesse, plowing through a small hotel. There was a huge ball of fire and an enormous plume of black smoke. Within minutes of the crash, dozens of fire engines and ambulances raced to the scene to tackle the blaze and search for survivors. But all 109 passengers and crew were killed, along with four people on the ground.

DEBRIS

Sections of the Relais Bleu hotel had been reduced to burning rubble and twisted metal. The blackened hulk of the Concorde was barely recognizable.

 EYEWITNESS

Sylvie Lucas was watching from an airport lounge as the plane took off. She thought the Concorde was on fire before it had even left the ground.

"The flames were coming from the back of the plane. We were waiting to hear the explosion because we thought it was going to fall here [at the airport]."

Gonesse, France, 2000

WHAT HAD HAPPENED?

A metal strip on the runway, which had fallen off a Continental Airlines DC-10, had burst one of the plane's tires. Parts of the burst tire hit the wing, puncturing a fuel tank. The leaking fuel caught fire. Unable to retract the undercarriage and with both engines one and two out of action, the pilots found it impossible to gain height. This made the crash unavoidable.

Flames trail behind the stricken aircraft in this dramatic newsreel photo.

RECURRENT PROBLEMS

This was the first crash in Concorde's 24 years of service. However tire bursts had been a regular problem for Concorde. A bad landing blew out a plane's tire in 1979. The incident led to a design modification.

A NEAR-MISS

In 1993 a Concorde tire blowout threw off a water deflector. The deflector pierced the fuel tank on a British Airways plane taxiing nearby. After that, the Air Accident Investigation Branch recommended changes. British Airways modified the wheel apparatus, but Air France did not.

WEAKNESSES WITH CONCORDE

The Paris crash came one day after British Airways confirmed hairline cracks had been discovered in the wings of all seven of its Concorde fleet. However, the Paris crash had nothing to do with these cracks. The Air France plane had been inspected a few days before and given a clean bill of health.

LEARNING FROM CATASTROPHES

After the Paris crash, British Airways and Air France grounded their fleet of Concordes. After extensive modifications, strengthening the tires and adding a protective liner to the fuel tank, they went back into service. But the disaster had shaken passengers' confidence in the plane. By 2003 British Airways and Air France decided it was too expensive to keep the planes flying. Concorde's last commercial passenger flight was on October 24, 2003.

The *Hindenburg* Disaster, 1937

The *Hindenburg* was the largest rigid airship ever built. At 804 feet (245 m) long, it was roughly the length of three jumbo jets parked end to end. It was named after Paul Hindenburg, World War I military leader and then President of Germany.

The Hindenberg *was the pride of Germany.*

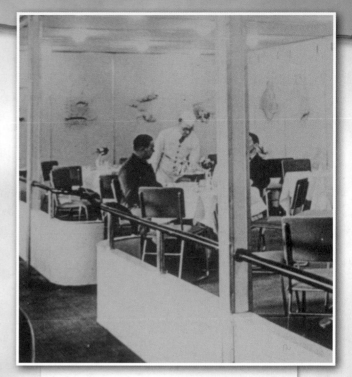

The interior of the airship was opulent and catered for only a small number of passengers.

SKY LINER

Hydrogen-filled German airships had been crossing the Atlantic regularly without mishap since 1928. With a top speed of 84 mph (135 kph), the *Hindenburg* could make the transatlantic trip in just 65 hours. By 1937, it had safely carried 1,002 passengers on ten round trips between Germany and the United States.

TRAVELING IN STYLE

The *Hindenburg* offered the same luxury as an ocean liner. Each of the 25 double cabins had hot and cold running water. The airship even had its own bar. Although it was lifted by explosive hydrogen, the *Hindenburg* had a smoking room, which was protected by a system of double doors. The only lighter on board was chained to the side of the room. Passengers had to hand over all their matches and cigarette lighters as they boarded the airship.

HELIUM AND THE THREAT OF WAR

Instead of using hydrogen, the designers had wanted to use the nonflammable gas helium. However, the United States—with the only significant stock of the inert gas—feared that German leader Adolf Hitler would use airships for military purposes if Germany had access to helium.

A SAFE MODE OF TRANSPORTATION?

On May 6, 1937, the *Hindenburg* left Frankfurt with 36 passengers and 61 crew on board. She made good time over the Atlantic and at around 7 PM on May 6, 1937, she arrived at Lakehurst and came into position beside her mooring mast.

FIRE!

At 7:25 PM, mooring ropes were thrown down to the ground crew and the engines were reversed for braking. Suddenly a huge flame shot out of the top of the *Hindenburg*.

THE DEATH TOLL

The huge airship then plummeted to the ground. The world-famous *Hindenburg* was consumed by the flames in little under a minute. Of the 97 passengers and crew on board, 35 died, along with one member of the ground crew.

Many claimed the explosion was the work of anti-Nazi saboteurs.

A huge flame shot out of the top of the Hindenburg as it moored in Lakehurst.

THE AFTERMATH

Although Germany continued to build airships after the *Hindenburg* tragedy, the United States continued to refuse to supply helium. Public confidence in airships was destroyed and with the coming of World War II in 1939, the remaining airships were broken up and their aluminum airframes used to make warplanes.

SABOTAGE?

Almost inevitably, there were mutterings of anti-Nazi sabotage, particularly from Hugo Eckener, a former head of the Zeppelin company. The *Hindenburg* was a status symbol for the Nazi regime, and was marked prominently with Nazi swastikas. However, no evidence was ever produced to support this view.

WHY DID IT HAPPEN?

A number of theories have been suggested to explain the end of the *Hindenburg*. One theory is that a snapped staywire pierced the skin, and static electricity had set fire to the escaping gas. Some historians have speculated that the covering of the skin of the *Hindenburg* caught fire. The skin was coated with a substance containing iron oxide and an aluminum acetate, both of which are very flammable. This theory seems unlikely, however, given the speed of the inferno's spread.

GUNMA PREFECTURE

Mountain Crash, 1985

On August 12, 1985, a Japan Airlines jumbo jet crashed into a mountain range, killing 517 passengers and crew, and making the accident the worst air crash involving a single plane.

DELAYED RESCUE EFFORTS

The plane had crashed at about 7 PM, just after it got dark. But the Japanese rescue workers did not arrive on the scene until dawn the following morning. The problem was that neither the civilian nor military rescue workers had access to the necessary night rescue equipment.

REJECTION OF HELP

U.S. military rescue teams at an American airbase less than half an hour away had night rescue equipment, which had been developed during the Vietnam War. American authorities informed the Japanese government that they had the equipment and the men sat up all night waiting for the call. But the U.S. offer of help was not accepted. This may have been a result of Japanese national pride.

SURVIVAL AGAINST THE ODDS

Miraculously there were three survivors. More could have been saved if the rescue team had arrived sooner—the three survivors heard the groans of other survivors. One even heard the cries of their father and sister who perished during the night.

Rescue workers explore the crash site.

Looking to the Future

Every time a plane crashes, officials try to learn lessons from the accident so that the same kind of disaster can be avoided in the future. This is why travel by plane is extremely safe. It is much safer, for example, than travel by car. It is precisely because plane crashes are unusual that they are so newsworthy when they happen.

FIRE SAFETY

Many of the accidents described in this book have led directly to improvements in safety. Modern planes are made with fire-retardant materials, so that fire will not spread so quickly. Another change that has resulted from crashes is that the layout inside planes has been altered to give people more time to escape in a fire.

AIR TRAFFIC CONTROL

Other accidents have led to changes in the way aircraft are guided through the air and on runways. The U.S. government set up the Federal Aviation Agency after a collision over the Grand Canyon in 1956. The agency was put in charge of all air traffic control systems in the United States.

OVERCOMING THE LANGUAGE BARRIER

The 1977 runway crash in Tenerife (see pages 10–11) resulted in all pilots being required to use standard English phrases when talking to air traffic control—no matter what part of the world they were operating in.

A pilot and his copilot take the controls of a modern aircraft.

Timeline

May 6, 1937, Lakehurst, New Jersey
The airship *Hindenburg* crashed to the ground in flames as she moored after a transatlantic journey, and was consumed by the flames.

March 3, 1974, near Paris, France
A McDonnell Douglas DC-10 operated by Turkish Airlines crashed into a forest outside Paris, resulting in 346 deaths. The cargo door had not been properly closed.

March 27, 1977, Tenerife
Two Boeing 747s collided on the runway at Rodeos Airport on Tenerife in the Canary Islands.

May 25, 1979, Chicago
The left-hand engine of an American Airlines DC-10 was torn off as it reached 400 feet (122 m). The plane smashed to the ground.

November 28, 1979, Antarctica
Flight 901 from Auckland Airport in New Zealand hit the side of Mount Erebus and disintegrated.

August 12, 1985, Japan
A Japan Airlines jumbo jet crashed into a mountain range, killing 517 passengers and crew.

January 1990, New York
A Boeing 707 crashed into woods after fuel ran out in mid-air. The pilots had been unable to communicate their fuel shortage to air traffic control.

December 1995, Cali, Colombia
An American Airlines plane crashed into a mountain while descending, killing 163 passengers and crew.

January 8, 1996, Kinshasa, Zaire (*the Democratic Republic of the Congo*)

At least 250 people were killed when a cargo plane crashed into a crowded street market.

July 17, 1996, Mid-Atlantic

A Trans World Airlines jumbo jet bound for Paris crashed into the Atlantic Ocean about a half hour after leaving Kennedy Airport in New York.

November 13, 1996, New Delhi

A Saudi 747 and a Kazakh Ilyushin Il-76 cargo plane collided in mid-air 60 miles (97 km) to the west of New Delhi.

July 25, 2000, Gonesse, France

Air France Concorde Flight AF4590 caught fire immediately after takeoff, and crashed near the town of Gonesse in an explosion.

September 11, 2001, New York

Four commercial airliners were hijacked by members of the terrorist organization, Al-Qaeda. Two of these were deliberately flown into the towers of the World Trade Center in New York. A third plane was flown into the Pentagon.

October 8, 2001, Milan, Italy

An SAS jet collided with a German Cessna on the runway at Milan Airport.

2 July, 2002, Lake Constance, Southern Germany

A Russian Tupolev 154 airliner carrying 95 people collided with a Boeing 757 cargo aircraft in mid-air.

Glossary

air traffic controller The trained ground-based workers who give pilots instructions.

charter A flight that is paid for by a company or individual, so that the passengers do not buy their tickets directly from the airline.

clearance The permission given to a pilot to proceed with an action, such as a takeoff or landing.

coalition A temporary union of countries or political parties that share a common goal.

control tower The building at an airport from which air traffic controllers instruct aircraft and other forms of transport on and around the airport.

coordinates A set of numbers that locate an aircraft on a map grid.

deck altitude alarm A warning given to a pilot if the aircraft is flying at a dangerous height.

electromagnetic pulses Bursts of an electric (or magnetic) force that can cause sparks.

flight recorder A machine that records a plane's flight data and/or the pilots' voices.

fuselage The main body of an aircraft which holds the passengers, crew and cargo.

holding pattern The flight path (usually circular) that an aircraft takes while waiting to land at an airport.

leading edge slat system The sets of flaps along the front edge of an aircraft's wings, moved to reduce or increase lift.

pylon A structure used to attach items such as fuel tanks to the body of an aircraft.

radar A system that uses radio waves to show the position of flying aircraft.

staywire Wires around an airship that are used to control an airship and hold it together.

taxiing The slow movement of an aircraft on the ground before takeoff or after landing.

undercarriage The landing gear (including wheels and tires) that a plane uses on a runway to land, take off and taxi.

water deflector A part of an aircraft designed to stop water damaging the aircraft when it lands.

Further Information

FURTHER READING

Spalding, Frank. *Plane Crash: True Stories of Survival.* New York, NY: Rosen Publishing Group, Inc, 2007.

Benoit, Peter. *The Hindenburg Disaster.* New York, NY: Scholastic, 2011.

Nahum, Andrew. *Eyewitness: Flight.* New York, NY: Dorling Kindersley, 2011.

Maynard, Christopher. *Machines at Work: Airplane.* New York, NY: Dorling Kindersley, 2006.

WEB SITES

Due to the changing nature of Internet links, Rosen Publishing has developed an online list of Web sites related to the subject of this book. This site is updated regularly. Please use this link to access this list:

http://www.rosenlinks.com/ cata/air

DVDs

Mayday: Air Disasters directed by Greg Lanning and Bryn Higgins (2003; DVD: 2009)

Miracle on the Hudson and Other Extraordinary Air Crash Events (2009)

Concorde Alpha-Delta: An Intrepid Journey (2005)

Index